The Simple Little

VEGAN DOG BOOK

CRUELTY-FREE RECIPES FOR CANINES

by Michelle A. Rivera

BOOK PUBLISHING COMPANY
Summertown, Tennessee

Library of Congress Cataloging-in-Publication Data

Rivera, Michelle A.
   The simple little vegan dog book : cruelty-free recipes for canines / by
Michelle A. Rivera.
      p.   cm.
   ISBN 978-1-57067-243-9
1. Dogs—Food—Recipes.   2. Vegan cookery.   I. Title.
   SF427.4.R58 2009
   636.7'085—dc22
                                                                          2009020812

Book Publishing Co. is a member of Green Press Initiative. We chose to print this title on paper with postconsumer recycled content, processed without chlorine, which saved the following natural resources:

34 trees

1,436 pounds of solid waste

12,313 gallons of wastewater

2,722 pounds of greenhouse gases

24 million BTU of total energy

For more information, visit www.greenpressinitiative.org.

Paper calculations from Environmental Defense Paper Calculator, www.edf.org/papercalculator.

Printed in Canada

Book Publishing Company
P.O. Box 99
Summertown, TN 38483
888-260-8458
www.bookpubco.com

ISBN: 978-1-57067-243-9

17 16 15 14 13 12 11 10 09   1 2 3 4 5 6 7 8 9

Contents

Foreword

A growing number of us are choosing a vegan lifestyle because we don't want to harm other animals and because we want to live in a way that is consistent with compassionate values and leaves a lighter footprint. Eating plant foods instead of animals is health promoting, humane, environmentally sustainable, and a denunciation of the cruel disrespect of other animals that has become rampant in our food system. Happily, with increasing awareness, there is a growing number of vegans in the United States and around the world.

If we wish to reject the environmental degradation and unnecessary exploitation and suffering of others to feed ourselves, why would we accept these abuses in order to feed our dogs? The food that we purchase for our nonhuman companions, just like the food we choose for ourselves, has a profound effect on the well-being of our planet and on the billions of animals killed by the food industry every year.

The dog-food business is inextricably linked to the factory-farming industry. The same animals (including both land and sea animals) that are used in human food are also used in our dogs' food. Purchasing commercial dog food supports brutal and irresponsible industries.

And animal products that end up in dog food can also pose threats to our companions. The alarming fact is that it is indeed legal for diseased animals to be used for human food, and the same is true when it comes to food for our animal companions. Tainted cuts of meat that are turned down for human food are routinely sent into the rendering system and then used in companion-animal products. There have even been accounts of euthanized dogs and cats being used in animal food, a concept that is a shock to the system.

Industrialized animal agriculture treats living creatures like mere commodities, subjecting them to torturous living conditions and brutal deaths. If we wish to promote compassion instead of cruelty and provide health-supporting food for our canine companions, we should steer clear of meat-based dog food. Doing so is good for our dogs and also for the animals that would otherwise have suffered and died for their consumption.

This book, *The Simple Little Vegan Dog Book*, is not meant to argue on behalf of a vegetarian lifestyle for your dog. There are many books that put forth the argument that dogs were never meant to be carnivores, or, alternatively, that feeding your dog a diet rich in plant-based proteins is not enough for him to thrive. We leave those arguments to another day. We believe that once you know the facts of life for animals on factory farms, it becomes difficult to continue to support that industry for food for yourself or your loved ones.

So we hope that you find this book useful in your quest for a nonviolent lifestyle for your canine family members. They, too, deserve to live cruelty free.

Gene Baur
PRESIDENT AND CO-FOUNDER,
FARM SANCTUARY

Preface

This was an enjoyable book to write, because people who have adopted a vegan diet for their dogs are motivated, positive, and ready to talk about their choices. The decision to put your dog on a vegan diet should never be made lightly, and we hope that you discuss your dog's specific nutritional needs with your veterinarian. After all, dogs are individuals, with individual needs, likes, and dislikes. What may be a perfect nutritional regimen for your Uncle Sal's dog may not be such a great choice for your own little munchkin. And even dogs living in the same "pack" (your household) may not all be candidates for a vegan diet.

This book is meant to be a tool for those who would like to learn a little about how to help their dog adopt a vegan diet. It is not meant as an argument for adopting a vegan diet, and it is not meant to provide you with copious research about why a vegan diet may be the best choice for your companion dog. There are plenty of other resources for the serious investigator.

I hope that by the time you come to this book you have already done your homework and learned all you can about canine nutrition and whether a vegan diet is good for your particular dog. Just as a cookbook is not designed to teach you about your body's nutritional needs, *The Simple Little Vegan Dog Book* is not designed to educate you as much as it is intended to spark your imagination and help you to find creative ways to feed your dog a nutritious alternative to commercial dog food.

Dogs are omnivores and, as such, they can eat a variety of wonderful foods, just like we humans can. So sit back and enjoy. I promise to keep it . . . simple.

Michelle Rivera
JUPITER, FLORIDA

Acknowledgments

Writing this book has been a fun journey, and I have met lots of lovely people along the way. I begin with my friend Lorraine Kassarjian, DVM, who has been an advocate of the vegan lifestyle for people for many years. Although she is not equally as positive about a vegan diet for dogs, she understands that people are passionate about their activism, and if that activism extends to their canine companions, well, she's all for it! I also want to thank my other veterinarian friend, Michael Berkenblit, who has been a great resource when I didn't understand some of the research I found and when I needed clarification on whether a certain food item was good for dogs or not. He's been an inspiration for me on all my literary projects and continues to be a valued friend.

My publisher, Cynthia Holzapfel, is always ready with a helpful suggestion, a quick answer, or an important decision and has been such a mentor for me. I love her enthusiasm and her lack of negativity. She's always ready to try something new, and for that I am deeply grateful. Also, I extend my heartfelt thanks to my editor, Jo Stepaniak, for her patience, kindness, and tolerance. Her hard work and dedication to perfection are both an inspiration and a delight. I would also like to thank Jason and Stephanie Clark for their friendship, advice, and recommendations, as well as Darren Middlesworth of V-dog for some really powerful information. Thanks, too, to the many people who shared with me their own experiences with their canine's journey toward a vegan diet, specifically Brad King and Fran Savarick. I also want to thank my daughter-in-law, Penny Rivera, who is a foodie and has been very helpful during this process. And of course, thanks to the rest of my family, especially my husband, for always being the constant in my life. They keep me centered and on track. But thanks most of all to my two canine companions, Murphy the golden retriever and Tabitha the standard poodle, who were all too eager to try the tasty treats offered herein.

The Simple Little

VEGAN DOG BOOK

CRUELTY-FREE RECIPES FOR CANINES

Introduction

Happiness is a warm puppy.

CHARLES M. SCHULZ

Imagine for a moment that you are invited to the home of an acquaintance, a person whom you don't know very well. You'd like to bring a hostess gift, but what? You don't know much about this person, so it's a tough call. You do recall, however, that someone mentioned there was a dog in the household. So you put together a lovely basket of beautifully decorated homemade dog biscuits and a pretty *peu de gâteau de chien* (little doggy cake). Of course, amid common bottles of wine and ho-hum layer cakes, your gift is unique and you've made a great impression. Who doesn't love someone who brings treats for the family dog? Anyone who walks into a stranger's house with biscuits for the resident canine has made a friend for life!

If the treats are cruelty-free, organic, and beautifully decorated, all the better. And once you explain that this is how your own dogs eat all the time, you'll be the envy of every dog lover in the room. This is always an impressive ice breaker.

So here it is—a little book about helping your dog to follow a plant-based diet. Maybe you already do, so why shouldn't he or she?

Current surveys show that the number of American households with vegetarians and vegans is growing every year. In my years of working as a veterinary technician, I have noticed that many people who follow the vegan way of life are full of vitality and curiosity; so of course they want that good health and vitality for their companion animals as well. Some veterinarians are steadfastly against vegan or even vegetarian diets for dogs. But there can be no doubt that even the ones who strongly believe that dogs require meat will consent, however grudgingly, to teaching their clients how to safely and healthfully switch their dogs to a vegan diet when they are persistent. For example, veterinarians may recommend the use of various supplements to compensate for whatever nutrients they feel the vegan diet is lacking. Nevertheless, the reluctance of veterinarians to get on board with a plant-based diet for their patients may be unfounded. In the Vegetarian Dog Health Survey conducted by People for the Ethical Treatment of Animals (PETA,) researchers concluded that 82 percent of the dogs that were fed a vegan diet were in "good to excellent health." Moreover, none of the dogs that had been on the diet for at least five years had illness of any kind, and overall there was a dramatic reduction in the number of dogs with ear infections, urinary tract infections, or eye infections. (See www.helpinganimals.com/h-vegcat-survey.html for more information on this study.)

It makes good sense that when you switch your dog from a high-fat diet composed of 4D meat (meat from animals that are dead, diseased, dying, or disabled) the result will be a happier and healthier companion. Dogs suffer from cancer, gastroenteritis, and a host of other diseases that may be the consequence of the foods they eat, just as it is with people. A change in diet, therefore, may be just what the doggy doctor ordered!

Not all vegans set out to change their dogs' diets. But many vegans find that, as they continue their own journey, it is difficult to open and serve a can of dog food that contains the remains of other animals—animals deemed unfit for human consumption. But when we look for more nutritious, premium dog food, we instead find fare composed of even more animals: kangaroos, rabbits, ducks, lamb, and fish. Could a vegan diet be the answer?

Rest assured, I am aware that dogs are omnivores and that many educated dog people believe wholeheartedly that dogs must have meat to survive. Some veterinarians believe that too. Here you will find interviews with veterinarians and animal nutrition enthusiasts so that you can draw your own conclusions. But the bottom line is, if you are motivated to feed your dog plant-based fare, you will find a way. We want to make sure the way you find is health-promoting for your dog.

While it's true that dogs need certain nutrients in order to thrive, the source of those nutrients is immaterial. There are easy ways to substitute a plant-based source for an animal-based one, and do so safely and deliciously.

Bear in mind that not all foods that are suitable for humans are safe for dogs to consume. I am so grateful that chocolate wasn't safety tested on dogs, because if it had been, the conclusion would have been that chocolate is toxic. While toxicity levels for certain foods can vary from dog to dog, some foods that we enjoy are dangerous or even deadly for canines.

For many of us, becoming vegan has been a process. Just as we have learned how to safely follow a plant-based diet, we can use our knowledge to help our dogs become healthy vegans too. This book will motivate you to use fresh ingredients that are suitable for everyone in the household to eat—including the humans. I once handed my four-year-old niece a bone-shaped biscuit I had made for my rescued greyhound, Eli. When the youngster joyfully bit into her "cookie," her shocked parents looked on in horror. What they didn't know is that the "dog" biscuit was made of wholesome grains and a little pumpkin—foods appropriate for humans and dogs alike.

The Vegan Lifestyle

The dog is a gentleman; I hope to go to his heaven, not man's.

MARK TWAIN

What Is a Vegan Lifestyle?

The words "vegetarian" and "vegan" are commonly used as nouns, as in "she is a vegetarian" or "he has decided to be a vegan." But they could also be used as adjectives, as in "she is following a vegetarian diet" or "he has decided to try a vegan lifestyle."

There is some confusion about the definitions of these terms. Followers of a vegan lifestyle are often asked what the difference is between a vegetarian and a vegan. The answer is easy. A vegetarian is a person who follows a plant-based diet and may also consume animal-derived foods, such as eggs, milk, cheese, yogurt, ice cream, and other dairy products. A vegan is a person who avoids all animal products both in diet and lifestyle and subscribes to a cruelty-free philosophy. Thus a vegan not only avoids meat, eggs, and dairy products, but also leather, silk, fur, feathers, honey, and cosmetics, pharmaceuticals, and any other products that include animal derivatives or that have been tested on animals. Although giving up meat in favor of a vegetarian diet is often done for health reasons, adopting a vegan diet is usually an ethical choice. There's no doubt that following a vegetarian diet can be healthful, or that following a vegan diet provides even greater health advantages. Thus we might think that if a plant-based diet is health-promoting for people, it would be health-promoting for dogs too, right?

Not so fast, says Lorraine Kassarjian, a veterinarian based in South Florida. Although Dr. Kassarjian believes a vegan diet is fine for people, she contends that dogs and cats need meat because they are carnivores, and carnivores cannot survive on leafy greens alone.

> Yes, you can raise your dog on a vegan diet, but you have to be very careful and make sure that your particular dog's system can process plant-based protein sources like soy products. A dog's body is different from ours. As carnivores, their intestines are shorter, and because of this, they may not get enough protein from plant-based sources.

> The way we know if an animal is a carnivore, herbivore, or omnivore, aside from watching them eat, is to look at their intestines. The length of an animal's intestines indicates what it needs to eat. Our bodies have to work harder to digest meat than grains due to our long, convoluted intestines. This is why some vegetarians argue that humans are natural herbivores. It is also why people who eat a lot of meat might get colon cancer and other diet-related diseases. Meat stays in our colons much longer than it should. But dogs have short intestines, and cats even shorter, so they are essentially built to live on protein. Dogs process meat better than they process tofu, which requires a longer digestion time. With dogs, most of their food heads right back out the other end, so the protein in tofu does not have much chance to get absorbed. People who put their dogs on a vegan

diet have to watch them closely to make sure they are not getting malnourished because they are not getting the right proteins. Dogs on a vegan diet should have their blood tested regularly to ensure they are receiving adequate nutrition.

If there are people who are willing to spend the time and effort to confirm their dogs are getting all the essential nutrients they need on a vegan diet, then I would tell them to proceed, with these words of caution: have the dog's blood checked on a regular basis, ensure the dog is eating as much as he should, and measure everything the dog is consuming.

Leonid Vidrivich, another South Florida veterinarian, has been practicing veterinary medicine for over thirty years. Like Dr. Kassarjian, he is a vegan, but he is not sure he would advocate a vegan diet for all dogs. He may, however, give his consent in certain situations. If an animal guardian is insisting on feeding his or her dog a plant-based diet, Dr. Vidrivich agrees that the owner needs to be educated about how to do it responsibly.

A balanced diet is the best for all animals. According to Traditional Chinese Medicine, diet is extremely important in developing personality. If an animal is deficient in a specific mineral, he needs the right food to address that problem. Certain foods are known to calm animals down; others may stimulate the dormant side of their behavior, similar to what alcohol does to humans. Of course, a lot depends on the breed, the living conditions, and what is expected of the dog. Dogs that are used for sledding, for example, live out in the snow in extreme temperatures. I'm not sure that a vegan diet would keep those dogs warm and healthy. They require meat to sustain them in those frigid, icy conditions. A Florida dog, however, may do very well on a vegan diet. So-called lap dogs probably don't need meat either, and neither do pampered dogs living in Upper Manhattan suites. These dogs expend very little energy throughout the day. Hard-working dogs have different needs; I think they may very well require some meat in their diets.

Dogs have a bouquet of personalities. At any given time they may show different sides of their personalities according to their genetic makeup, the foods they are eating, and the people they are interacting with. A variety of factors can be responsible for bringing out personality traits in a dog. Some people advocate a raw meat diet. But raw meat can have an undesirable effect on dogs—it can expose their aggressive side. Look at the diet of human beings who fight for a living, such as boxers and wrestlers. They eat a lot of meat, which I believe provokes their personality type. Vegan food may have a calming effect on dogs, and that is encouraged, as it maintains a state of homeostasis. I can agree with feeding dogs a vegan diet, but only if it is done carefully. The dog's owner must ensure that the food is high quality and contains all the elements the dog needs to be healthy. I can live with that.

Dr. Vidrivich has an atypical perspective compared to most veterinarians, because he has been a shelter vet for many years. Shelter medicine is very different from private veterinary practices, because the animals that come to the shelter bring with them a myriad of problems that may be related to poor nutrition or a lack of food. His opinion on the subject of vegan dogs may have developed from seeing how dogs respond to food when they have not had it for a while, or when the food they have been given is inconsistent with their needs. On the other hand, adopted animals are typically well cared for and their dietary issues are usually linked to food allergies and the occasional tummy troubles caused by eating something they shouldn't have.

Darren Middlesworth, co-owner of V-dog, has a solution that may make vegans, their dogs, and Dr. Kassarjian and Dr. Vidrivich happy. "Our company provides vegan dog food that has been formulated to ensure that dogs get everything they need in terms of proteins, vitamins, and minerals. We work very closely with a veterinarian who has done research on how to safely implement a vegan diet for dogs, and we feel confident that dogs can obtain all the nutrients they need from our product."

V-dog has only been in business for about six years, but they are using the same formula as a British vegan dog food company, Happy Dog, which has been in business for thirty years and has fed ten generations of dogs. "We've even heard of one dog that lived to be twenty-seven years old being fed nothing but a vegan diet. We are always happy to hear stories like that," says Darren.

What about supplementing the vegan food with vitamins in pill form? "You can't really supplement a meat-free diet with vitamins," says Dr. Kassarjian. "Only about 2 percent of the vitamins in pill form get absorbed. There is no such thing as a protein pill for dogs, and that's the problem; dogs have a much higher need for protein than we do."

But there is a solution! If you use a commercially prepared vegan dog food, the necessary nutrients have already been added for you. And if you want to give your dog some variety, there are easy ways to diversify his diet, which I discuss later in this book. If you are seeking simplicity while maintaining your dog's health, purchasing commercial kibble will certainly be much simpler than cooking for your dog every day.

Make sure that you and your veterinarian are in sync with your decision to help your dog "go veg." Several of the veterinarians I've spoken with in clinics around the country told me that many of their clients are asking about vegan diets for their dogs. As more and more people become aware of the benefits of a vegan lifestyle for themselves, they are also beginning to ask if it is possible to bring their dog into their circle of cruelty-free living.

With the recent recalls of so many dangerous and contaminated products, from children's toys to motor vehicles, from meat products to vegetables, and from peanut butter to pet food, consumers are rightfully wary about product safety. If the food that is considered safe for human consumption can no longer be trusted, what does that say about the meat that goes into commercial pet foods? Furthermore, exactly what *is* the meat that goes into these products?

We are all aware of the ubiquitous "meat by-products" that is listed on commercial pet food labels. That ingredient is a large part of what your dog is eating when you serve him standard pet food products. "Meat by-products" refers to the parts that are left after an animal has been rendered. This may include the head, viscera, neck, bones, feet, intestines, eyes, nose, tail, and, in the case of poultry, feathers. According to the Association of American Feed Control Officials (AAFCO), "meat by-products" is defined as the "non-rendered, clean parts, other than meat, derived from slaughtered mammals. It includes, but is not limited to, blood, lungs, spleen, kidneys, brain, livers, blood, bone, partially defatted low-temperature fatty tissue, and stomachs and intestines freed of their contents. It does not include hair, horns, teeth, and hoofs." According to the AAFCO, it is suitable for use in animal food.

According to law, the by-products listed on dog food labels need not be named individually. Of course, they wouldn't be, because the gross-out factor would put any thinking person into a tailspin. As long as the ingredients of the by-products correspond to the definition above (from the AAFCO), the product is not required to contain meat from any specific animal. Some activist insiders claim that even dogs and cats end up in pet food as meat by-products.

Since there is virtually no oversight of 4D meat, it is possible that the animals used for it have died of undiagnosed bacterial or viral infections. Pet food has been part of the occasional meat recalls due to mad cow disease (bovine spongiform encephalopathy, also known as BSE). The only silver lining in the aftermath of these massive recalls is that companion animal owners are more discerning about what they feed their pets, leading to a greater demand for high-quality, organic, chemical-free pet food.

If the apprehension over 4D meats is not enough to make consumers question the use of commercial pet food, there are also valid concerns over the preservatives used to keep the food looking fresh, moist, and colorful. Two commonly used preservatives are butylated hydroxyl toluene (BHT) and butylated hydroxyanisole (BHA). Ethoxyquin, commonly used as a pesticide, is also widely used in dog food. A pesticide! Incredibly, ethoxyquin is the preservative that causes the most concern, because there is so much of it in pet food. The law allows 150 parts per million (ppm), much higher than other preservatives. Over the past decade, there has been increased scrutiny of the addition of ethoxyquin to pet food because of reports of canine health issues. BHT is an additive used not only in dog food but also in the manufacture of cosmetics, pharmaceuticals, jet fuel, rubber, petroleum, and embalming. Yes, embalming fluid. According to the National Institutes of Health, BHA is "reasonably anticipated to be a human carcinogen." Every year, it seems, we are learning about a new danger lurking in pet food. In 2007, it was melamine, a component in pesticides and fertilizers that killed some household pets, sickened thousands more, and caused the recall of millions of units of pet food. And who could forget when millions of pet food products and chew toys made in China were recalled after thousands of pets were sickened and died due to additives containing contaminated gluten. Since your dog is probably eating the same foods day after day, these toxic preservatives and chemicals are building up in her system over time, and her body never has an opportunity to cleanse itself of them.

Diet and the Environment

There are definite health benefits to a vegan diet. The risk of heart disease and cancer, both linked to the consumption of meat and animal products, is greatly minimized with a diet rich in vegetables and fruits. A plant-based diet is also beneficial to the environment. According to the United States Department of Agriculture, "The two biggest environmental problems with animal manures are ammonia evaporation into the atmosphere and phosphorus runoff into lakes and rivers. When ammonia evaporates from manure it not only causes poor animal production, due to high levels of ammonia in animal rearing facilities; it causes acid rain and other atmospheric pollution. Phosphorus runoff causes excessive algal blooms." Thus the inordinate amount of manure produced on today's factory farms has directly contributed to both acid rain and the destruction of aquatic ecosystems.

Consider these staggering facts: It takes 2,500 gallons of water to make just one pound of beef and 750 gallons of water to produce one gallon of milk. Simply by eating a plant-based diet, vegans can reduce their water consumption by 1.3 million gallons per year.

Due to the huge demand for meat, eggs, and dairy products, modern factory farms have replaced small family farms, which have rapidly disappeared. Countless acres of animal habitats and rain forests have been destroyed to make room for animal grazing lands. This mass production of animal products for food contributes more to global warming than all the pollution caused by the manufacture and use of planes, cars, and trucks combined.

Should I Introduce My Dog to a Vegan Diet?

Jason Clark has been feeding his dogs a vegan diet for over five years. He considers himself somewhat of an expert on the subject, having extensively studied and researched canine nutritional needs. He wanted to be absolutely sure he was providing the safest diet for his dogs. I asked him about the protein requirements for dogs, since that seems to be the sticking point for most people.

Protein is a very controversial subject when discussing nutritional needs. I think you have to look at an animal's natural diet and work backward. For example, humans were heavy fruit eaters, and possibly total fruitarians, millions of years ago. If humans are able to attain optimal health with a diet based almost exclusively on fruit, it would put our protein needs at approximately 10 percent of our caloric intake.

The domestic dog has been genetically manipulated by humans for hundreds of years. We could look at their wild ancestors, the wolf and coyote, as points of reference. Members of the canine family are carnivorous omnivores, so we know they can and will eat a variety of foods. Yes, other animals comprise a majority of their diet, but they consume them in a way that differs significantly from how humans consume other animals. Coyotes and wolves generally eat other animals that are heavy grazers of plant foods, such as rabbits, prairie dogs, and deer. When they begin eating, they usually start with the internal organs, the stomach and intestines, which contain partially digested vegetation. The muscle meat is last to be eaten before the bones. Therefore, they instinctively consume the least protein-dense part of the animal first; this is where the best nutrients are.

And while we are on the subject of coyotes, there is evidence that coyotes in certain parts of the country are primarily vegetarian. In *The Coyote: Defiant Songdog of the West* by Francois Leydet, the author states that an unpublished study by Robert D. Ohmart and Bertin W. Anderson of Arizona State University found that coyotes along the lower Colorado River could be primarily vegetarian. In the fall of 1974, honey mesquite and screwbean mesquite pods formed four-fifths of the bulk of their scats.

Although protein seems to be the major concern regarding a vegan diet for domestic dogs, virtually all plant foods contains some protein, although some have more than others. Table 1 lists the percentage of

TABLE 1 *Percentage of protein in various plant foods*

PLANT FOOD	PERCENTAGE OF PROTEIN	PLANT FOOD	PERCENTAGE OF PROTEIN
apples	1%	green peas	30%
apricots	8%	oranges	8%
blueberries	3%	peaches	6%
cantaloupe	9%	pears	5%
carrots	6%	prunes	4%
cherries	8%	pumpkin	2%
figs	6%	sweet peppers	22%
green beans	26%	watermelon	8%

dietary protein in a variety of plant foods. All of the foods listed are suitable and safe for dogs to consume.

Naturally, when you mix fruits and/or vegetables with other foods that are high in protein, such as peanut butter (which dogs love), you can double or triple the amount of protein. Spreading peanut butter on apple slices, figs, or watermelon chunks, or blending pumpkin and peanut butter together, will raise the protein count much higher. And while it's fine to mix some peanut butter into your dog's food (watch that fat content), take care with adding herbs and spices such as thyme, garlic powder, or seasoning blends to your homemade products. These added flavorings are often unnecessary.

"I have seven vegan dogs," says Jason. "One of my dogs always waits for the leftover piece of tomato when we slice one, but the rest of them will not eat tomato. A couple of my dogs like a variety of vegetables, while most will not eat some of them. One of my dogs loves dried fruit for breakfast, but she does not always like fresh, ripe fruit. For example, she will not eat fresh blueberries but likes dried blueberries."

Jason cautions that it's best to be prepared for a lot of trial and error when switching your dogs to a vegan diet. "I have found that my dogs have almost individual tastes or texture preferences. I am currently trying to see if one of my dogs likes carrots. I have tried chunks of carrots and shredded carrots without success. My next step will be to try cooked carrots. As my dogs' diets continue to evolve, I would like to include mostly fruits, vegetables, and nuts, with a commercial vegan dog food as a supplement."

Although Jason Clark studied vegan dog nutrition as a project, making it a part-time job for himself, others have simply decided to try it and see how well it works for their dogs. Naturally, vegans care about the health of their animal companions, but while Jason feeds his dogs a plant-based diet strictly out of nutritional considerations, others are searching for a more ethical, kinder diet for their canine friends. One veterinarian I spoke with maintains that feeding dogs a plant-based diet will make them less aggressive, since bloodlust no longer factors into their food.

Fran Savarick of Plantation, Florida, swears by her dogs' diet:

Both my husband and I are vegan, so I decided that my dogs should be vegans too. I mean, why would I feed them something I wouldn't eat? When I learned about all the horrible ingredients that go into most commercial dog food—the 4D meats, road kill, and even other dogs and cats—and then heard the news that IAMS tests on animals, well, it was settled. I was determined not to feed that stuff to my dogs.

Both of my dogs have done well on a vegan diet. Taylor had a little arthritis, but he lived to be fifteen years old. That's quite a lifetime for a Labrador. He died of old age. I incorporate a mixture of commercial vegan dog foods like V-dog and biscuits by Wow-Bow and then supplement them with cooked lentils and carrots and other vegetables for texture and flavor. It was terrible when the news came out about the pet food from China being tainted with ingredients that were killing our dogs and cats, but I was relieved that I didn't have to worry about that at all. My dogs were safe.

Although adopting a vegan diet was an ethical decision for us, I know it is also better for our health. I try to be more holistic with my dogs, too. I feel good knowing that I am doing the best I can for them. I like to use the word "clean" when referring to our diet and way of life.

My veterinarian didn't have a problem with our desire to put our dogs on a vegan diet; he told me to go ahead and give it a try. But my friends said that it wouldn't work; they said that dogs are carnivores and it's not natural for them to be vegan. But how natural is it to wake up in the morning to a bowl of dry kibble? Dogs in the wild didn't have kibble. That's not natural either.

Jason agrees that diet can have a big impact on specific health concerns. One of his seven dogs is a cancer survivor, and Jason believes that her diet is an important factor in her still being with them.

My wife Stephanie and I adopted her when she was about a year old. By the time she was two she had a large lump growing on her side. A grapefruit-size tumor and the surrounding tissue were removed; the tumor was cancerous. We were told that because of the type of cancer it was, it could return at any time, in the same spot or anyplace else in her body, and we should be prepared that she may not make it to an old age. . . . She will be nine this winter.

Jason tells the story of another dog, this one a breeding dog rescued from a Missouri puppy mill.

He began having seizures. Along with keeping him hydrated, we learned to keep him away from BHT and BHA, which is found in many pet treats as well as pet foods. We also tried a vegan diet, with an emphasis on fruits and vegetables because of their high water content. We found that our efforts have paid off, as he has not had a seizure since.

So you don't have to convince Jason and his wife, a humane education coordinator with the Humane Society of the United States, of the value of a vegan diet for dogs. They know firsthand of its benefits and are happy to tell their story to anyone who will listen.

Brad King has William, a Chihuahua and terrier mix, who is about twelve years old. William has been eating vegan food since he was two. Why does Brad do it? "Feeding him animal products is not something I could do," Brad says. "Besides, I think William is meat intolerant anyway." Meat intolerant? Brad clarifies: "Dogs, especially older dogs, often have trouble digesting animal products. Chihuahuas, for example, were known to have originally eaten fresh fish, nuts, and berries."

Although I had not heard of this before, it makes sense; after all, not even the most strapping brute of a Chihuahua could be expected to bring down a buffalo or even a large squirrel. Not even an entire pack of Chihuahuas would be capable of hunting big game.

Brad continues, "Researchers found that early Chihuahuas had evidence of plant materials in their digestive system."

That is all very interesting, but how did he learn that his dog has an intolerance to meat? Surely William is not modeling the behavior he sees in his guardian, is he?

Surprisingly, there are plenty of dogs who suffer from terrible gastric distress, and it's quite possible the cause is meat, as was the culprit in poor little William's case. "We took away everything and started from nothing," explains Brad. "After that, we began reintroducing foods to him little by little. Turns out, we discovered that meat was causing the problem. He's been on a vegan diet ever since and has not had any gastric issues after we eliminated meat from his diet. We give him treats of vegan "chicken" strips and add cooked lentils to his food."

Because his person was enlightened enough to look into switching him from a meat-based diet to a plant-based one, William was one lucky canine. My Tabitha did not have cancer, thankfully, or even a meat-intolerance issue. No, her problem, like that of all standard poodles, was chronic ear infections. Sometimes the ear infection is bacterial, sometimes fungal, but it is always painful and difficult to treat. I tried all the flushes, drops, shots, and pills that are available, but nothing worked. Her veterinarian put her on one special diet after another in the hope that the chronic nature of the ear infection indicated a food allergy. There were times when it improved, but it never truly went away. In desperation, I decided to try her on a vegan diet. I started with a bag of V-dog, and later began cooking for her. I'm happy to report that Tabitha's' ears are much improved, and I can't help but feel that the change from a meat-based diet to a plant-based diet had something to do with it.

A Word about Cats

Cats are obligate carnivores and, as such, are not good candidates for a vegan diet. There are people who insist that their cats are doing quite well on a vegan diet, but it takes a great deal of risk and work on the part of the owner. Cats need taurine, an amino acid that is only produced by other animals. Taurine is harvested from the testicles of mammals; it is also found in the small intestine of many animals, including humans. But there is a synthetic taurine substitute, and it is commonly used in ordinary products such as energy drinks and contact lens solutions. Taurine is an essential nutrient for both humans and animals, as it has been proven to lower blood pressure, decrease blood sugar, and assist in keeping the central nervous system in a state of homeostasis.

Humans have the ability to synthesize the artificial compound, but unfortunately, cats do not have that capability. The absence of taurine in a cat's diet causes deterioration of the retina, leading to a condition called macular degeneration and, eventually, irreversible blindness. Additionally, without taurine, cats suffer alopecia (hair loss), tooth decay, and cardiomyopathy, a heart condition. Because it is so important to feline health, the Association of American Feed Control Officials (AAFCO) requires the addition of natural taurine in all pet food for cats, both wet and dry. Weighing the risks versus the benefits, I am not sure that putting my cat on a vegan diet is worth the danger of exposing him to some very serious health issues. Perhaps some cats can thrive on a vegan diet supplemented with synthetic taurine, but that's an argument that is beyond the scope of this book.

Hazardous and Safe Ingredients

The average dog is a nicer person than the average person.

ANDY ROONEY

Foods to Avoid

So, you've decided to try it! You have had a deep philosophical discussion with your dog, and you both have decided that the timing is right, and your dog couldn't agree more that killing animals for other animals to live is not the way to go. Good for both of you!

Before we get into the kinds of products you may want to keep on hand in your pantry, let's talk about things that, according to the

ASPCA, your dog should never have. It probably goes without saying that you shouldn't allow your dog to sip martinis with you; whether shaken or stirred, alcohol is number one on the do-not-have list. Animal fat is bad too, but I am assuming that since you are reading this book, you are not prone to trimming off the fat from your steak and feeding it to your dog. If you are, stop it right away! And fried foods are just as bad for your dog as they are for you. These kinds of saturated fats wreak havoc on the pancreas and can lead to pancreatitis, a life-threatening and painful condition.

Guacamole is great for chip dipping and salads, but since avocado can be harmful to your little furry friend, it's one "people food" he has to avoid. The avocado tree as well as the pit inside the avocado are toxic to dogs. Contact with the pit or the bark of the tree has been known to cause difficulty in breathing.

No bones about it, beef bones are out of bounds. It may be a well-known fact that chicken bones are bad for your dog, but the truth is that all bones can splinter and cause damage to your dog's esophagus, stomach, and intestines. Stick with faux bones, such as those made by Nylabone, instead.

Then there's chocolate. How convenient that America's favorite food is bad for dogs. That means there's more for us! Chocolate contains a bitter, volatile compound called theobromine. Theobromine is an alkaloid that affects us in much the same way as caffeine. In dogs, however, it can cause seizures, elevated blood pressure, coma, and, in extreme cases, death. Unsweetened chocolate, also called baking chocolate, is the most concentrated and thus the most dangerous, but it's probably best to avoid giving your dog chocolate of any kind. The same is true for products that contain caffeine, as they cause the same problems for dogs as chocolate.

Cold cuts are high in sodium and nitrates, which can cause digestive troubles as well as kidney issues. Never give cold cuts or any other highly processed meats to your dog.

Garlic and onions will not only make your dog's breath clear a room, in quantity they are dangerous for dogs. These decidedly aromatic root vegetables are high in sulfoxides and disulfides, which can destroy healthy erythrocytes (red blood cells) in dogs, leading to anemia.

Grapes and raisins, which are probably not palatable to most dogs anyway, are dangerous. They have been known to cause kidney failure even in small amounts.

Some nuts, particularly macadamias and walnuts, are off limits. The high phosphorous content in these nuts may lead to bladder stones and can cause weakness, muscle tremors, and paralysis. Note that peanut butter is listed among the "good" foods for dogs to eat; however, peanuts are technically a legume (bean), not a nut. Always purchase organic, sugar-free, unsalted peanut butter. Excessive salt can lead to electrolyte imbalances and bladder and kidney issues. Excessive sugar, in the form of white crystals or corn syrup, can contribute to obesity (with its attendant hip and other joint problems), diabetes, and dental caries. Xylitol, a sugar substitute found in gum and other artificially sweetened products, is extremely unsafe for dogs, as it can cause a sudden drop in blood sugar and, in large doses, is also toxic to the liver. You may be tempted to sweeten your dog's homemade vegan food, but resist the urge. Even if your dog begs every time you eat a candy bar or cookie, remember that he does not have the sweet tooth we humans have and adding unnecessary sweetening agents to his food is harmful and unnecessary.

Mushrooms, especially wild mushrooms, can be very dangerous to dogs. Although most dogs aren't interested in wild mushrooms, if you are out walking together and encounter a patch, it's best to steer clear of it.

Tomatoes have been linked to heart arrhythmias in dogs. Avoid giving your canine friend tomatoes, tomato sauce, and foods that contain tomato products, except in small amounts.

Never season your dog's food with nutmeg. Nutmeg has been linked to tremors and seizures in dogs, and even death.

Harmful Foods and Ingredients

alcohol	fried foods	nutmeg	salt
avocados	garlic	nuts	sugar
chocolate	grapes	onions	tomatoes
cold cuts	mushrooms	raisins	xylitol

While it's fine to add sliced or diced fruits—such as apples, peaches, or pears—to your pooch's meals, never give her the entire fruit to eat. Pits and seeds contain cyanide, a deadly toxin that can kill dogs (and people).

Non-Food Hazards

Even though you are vegan and are serving your dog vegan food, you still might be purchasing nonvegan chew toys. Avoid rawhide chew sticks in the shape of bones, strips, knots, and rolls. After your dog chews these for a while, they will become soft, gloppy, and sticky. Large chunks of these chew toys can then easily become lodged in your dog's throat and pose a choking hazard. As the rawhide is swallowed, it can scrape and irritate the throat, causing small lacerations where bacteria can build up. Once the rawhide reaches the stomach or lower intestinal tract, larger pieces can cause obstruction. Because the material is gluey, it can clump, forming a mass in the intestines that might need to be surgically removed. Furthermore, these chew toys are processed with a preservative that contains arsenic, and there have been recalls of some of these products due to salmonella contamination.

Cows' hooves are also hazardous. They are much too hard to chew, and a tooth can easily be broken while the dog is attempting to chew on one. When the hooves are severed, they break into shards, like glass fragments, which can cause severe bleeding or obstruction. Bowel perforation is an additional risk, and once that has happened, the resulting infection from the leakage of bowel contents can be deadly.

Pigs' ears and bulls' penises (marketed as "bully sticks") have the same dangers as rawhide chews. In addition, pigs' ears are typically contaminated with salmonella, posing a risk to you as well as your dog.

These toys pose so much risk, and there are safer, vegan choices available. Good options include Booda Bones, cornstarch-based bones for dogs, or toys such as tightly twisted ropes with knots on each end. Although the cotton threads may break off and be ingested, they are harmless and will pass through your dog's delicate intestines without harm. The threads also act as doggie dental floss when chewed.

Nylabone chew toys, which are made of hard but safe nylon, are nearly impossible to damage. Kong toys are also safe and fun. Try stuffing them with homemade biscuits and peanut butter.

Foods to Include

Other than these few exceptions, your dog is welcome to eat virtually everything you do, which gives you plenty of options to choose from. You may be surprised at the healthful ingredients you can use if you want to get creative and think outside the dog food box: pumpkin, brown rice, leafy greens, lentils, barley, and so much more!

Plain canned pumpkin (not the pie filling) is a rich, tasty addition to any dog's dinner. Pumpkin is frequently given to retired, rescued greyhounds, because when they are kenneled at the track their diet consists solely of raw meat. Pumpkin adds variety and fiber and is packed with vitamins and minerals. It is particularly high in beta-carotene, which is good for the eyes and is a superhero among vitamins for boosting the immune system. Carrots are also an excellent source of beta-carotene, the nutrient responsible for giving both carrots and pumpkin their orange color.

Brown rice is an outstanding addition to any dog's diet. I include it in a number of the recipes in this book, and you can also add it to commercial vegan dog food. Brown rice is a natural source of folate, riboflavin, magnesium, and iron, and it has three times the fiber found in white rice.

Why is fiber important in your dog's diet? Just as with our own diets, fiber keeps the bowels healthy and assists with regulating cholesterol levels. Dietary fiber helps firm up stools that are too loose (diarrhea), inhibits the lodgment of feces (impaction), and prevents hard stools (constipation). Extra fiber absorbs extra fluids, so be sure to always offer your dog plenty of fresh, clean water to accompany his fiber-rich feast.

Food Appearance and Safety

With all the wonderful ingredients you can put in your dogs' food, the color is likely to range from a bland gray to a deep orange to a milky white. Unless you are making biscuits to give as gifts and a beautiful presentation is important, don't be tempted to add any food coloring, especially red dye, as it is a known carcinogen that is banned in Europe. Unfortunately, red dye is routinely added to commercial pet food products to make them appear fresher and more appetizing. Check pet food labels very carefully to be sure red dye is not one of the additives listed.

If your dog's food shows any sign of mold or spoilage, no matter how small, throw it out. Spoiled food is just as harmful to dogs as it is for people.

Since this is a vegan book, I will not be advocating the addition of raw eggs to your dog's cuisine. However, if you are tempted to do so, remember that raw eggs carry salmonella.

Getting Started

No one appreciates the very special genius of your conversation as the dog does.

CHRISTOPHER MORLEY

Useful Equipment

The same kitchen equipment and tools that you use to prepare your own food are suitable for preparing your dog's food, too. Pots, pans, mixing bowls, and measuring spoons will all come in handy. A blender or small food processor will be useful as well. You don't need anything fancy; a small countertop model will do just fine.

Portion Size

Each recipe's yield will fluctuate depending on the size of the portions you give your dog. Obviously, large dogs need more food than small dogs, and their portion sizes will vary accordingly. A biscuit recipe may yield two dozen biscuits or twice that amount, depending on how large you make them and the size your dog prefers. You will need to experiment to determine the right portions for your particular dog's need.

Staple Ingredients

You will find that many of the recipes in this book call for staple ingredients such as rice, beans, lentils, barley, and oats. The following instructions will guide you in preparing these ingredients so that you can buy them in bulk and cook and freeze them for later use. This is a thrifty way to use these ingredients, and making food at home ensures it is sodium free. Because advance preparation will save you time and energy, it is highly recommended.

Beans

Dried beans are inexpensive and naturally low in sodium. If you prefer, you can use canned beans for the recipes in this book. They are convenient but higher in sodium, so please be sure to rinse them well before using to wash away the excess salt.

> 3 to 4 cups water
> 1½ cups dried beans *(red, white, or black)*
> 1 to 2 tablespoons olive oil *(optional)*
> Pinch salt

Combine the beans and water in a large pot and bring to a boil. Reduce the heat to medium and simmer briskly for 2 minutes. Remove from the heat and let rest, uncovered, for 1 hour. Drain the beans in a colander.

Transfer the drained beans to a clean, large pot and cover them with at least 6 cups of fresh water (the water should rise above the beans by at least 1 inch.) Add the optional oil (it will help prevent foaming) and the salt. Bring to a boil, lower the heat, and simmer uncovered for 1½ to 2 hours, or until tender. Add more hot water as needed to keep the beans covered with liquid as they cook.

Stored in an airtight container with their liquid, cooked beans will keep for 4 to 5 days in the refrigerator or 2 to 3 months in the freezer. For ease of use, freeze beans in 1- to 2-cup portions. Thaw frozen beans before using.

Rice

2 1/4 cups water

1 cup rice *(brown or white)*

To cook on the stovetop, bring the water to a boil in a medium saucepan. Stir in the rice, cover, and reduce the heat to low. Cook for 15 to 20 minutes for white rice or 45 minutes for brown rice, or until all of the water has been absorbed. Do not lift the lid while the rice is cooking. Let stand for 10 to 15 minutes. Remove the lid and fluff with a fork.

To cook in the microwave, combine the water and rice in a 2-quart microwave-safe casserole dish with a tight-fitting cover. Microwave on medium-high (80 percent power) for 20 minutes. Let stand for 5 minutes. Remove the cover and fluff with a fork.

Stored in sealed containers or zipper-lock bags, cooked rice will keep for 5 to 7 days in the refrigerator or 6 months in the freezer.

Lentils

Cook the lentils longer, until they are very soft, if you want to use them in a loaf or casserole. Alternatively, cook them a shorter time so they retain some firmness, if you want to sprinkle them on top of other foods.

> 1 cup dried lentils
>
> 1 ½ cups water or unsalted vegetable broth

Spread the lentils in a single layer on a white towel or light-colored surface. Sort through them and discard any foreign objects, such as pebbles, dirt, or twigs. Place the lentils in a strainer and rinse them thoroughly.

Bring the water to a boil in a medium saucepan and stir in the lentils. Boil for 3 minutes. Lower the heat and simmer uncovered until tender, about 30 minutes.

Drained and stored in sealed containers or zipper-lock bags, cooked lentils will keep for 7 days in the refrigerator or 6 months in the freezer.

Barley

YIELD: 3 CUPS

2 cups water

1 cup quick-cooking barley

Bring the water to a boil in a medium saucepan. Stir in the barley, cover, and reduce the heat to low. Cook for 10 to 13 minutes, or until tender. Remove from the heat and let stand for 5 minutes.

Stored in sealed containers or zipper-lock bags, cooked barley will keep for 5 to 7 days in the refrigerator or 6 months in the freezer.

Oatmeal

1 ¼ cups water

1 cup rolled oats

To cook on the stovetop, bring the water to a boil in a medium saucepan and stir in the oats. Cook on medium heat, stirring occasionally, for 5 minutes. Remove from the heat, cover, and let stand until cool.

To cook in the microwave, combine the water and oats in a 2-cup microwave-safe bowl. Microwave on medium (50 percent power) for 5 to 6 minutes. Stir well.

Stored in a sealed container in the refrigerator, oatmeal will keep for 14 days.

Shopping List

apples	nutritional yeast flakes
applesauce	oat flour
baking powder	peaches
baking soda	potatoes
bananas	pumpkin, unsweetened canned
barley, quick-cooking	rolled oats
beans, dried	soy yogurt
broccoli	spinach
brown gravy, vegan canned	sweet potatoes
brown rice	tofu, firm
bulgur	tomato sauce*
carrots	tortillas, flour
celery	vanilla extract
cornmeal	vegetable broth or bouillon cubes
cornstarch	vegetables, assorted
garlic powder*	unbleached white flour
green beans	whole wheat flour
lentils, dried	zucchini

*use only in small amounts

41

Biscuits

No philosophers so thoroughly comprehend us as dogs and horses.

HERMAN MELVILLE

When you make your own dog biscuits from healthful, plant-based, human-grade ingredients, you can be assured that your beloved friend is getting the freshest, tastiest, and most wholesome treats possible. Whenever you can, choose organic ingredients to further protect your dog's health and safeguard the environment in the process. An added benefit to making homemade biscuits is that you can adapt them to create all the flavors your dog especially loves. Cut them into bone shapes or other fun and fanciful designs that will make you both smile.

Yeasted Gourmet Dog Treats

This recipe especially suits the epicurean canine. These biscuits are somewhat lighter than Basic Vegan Dog Biscuits (page 46) because they are made with active dry yeast, which gives them a little rise.

1 package active dry yeast

3 1/2 cups salt-free vegetable broth

3 1/2 cups unbleached white flour

2 cups whole wheat flour

1 cup cornmeal

1/2 cup plain soymilk

Olive oil *(optional)*

Preheat the oven to 300 degrees F. Lightly oil 2 or 3 baking sheets. Dissolve the yeast in the broth and let rest for 10 minutes.

Combine the white flour, whole wheat flour, and cornmeal in a large mixing bowl. Add the broth mixture and soymilk and knead into a firm dough. Roll out the dough to a thickness of 1/4 inch and cut it into the shape of your choice using a cookie cutter or the rim of a drinking glass. Arrange on the prepared baking sheets. For a shiny appearance, brush the biscuits with olive oil.

Bake for 45 minutes. Turn the oven off but do not remove the biscuits. Allow the biscuits to cool in the oven for 8 to 12 hours, until they are hard and crunchy.

Stored in sealed containers or zipper-lock bags, Yeasted Gourmet Dog Treats will keep for 5 to 7 days at room temperature or 12 months in the freezer.

Basic Vegan Dog Biscuits

YIELD: 40 (2-inch) BISCUITS, OR 30 (3-inch) BISCUITS

It's easy to make homemade dog biscuits. This recipe gives you the basics, but feel free to experiment by adding flavorings to the biscuit dough—such as dried herbs, shredded carrots or other vegetables, or peanut butter—or try coloring them with drops of natural food coloring. To make the biscuits festive and more like cookies, press some carob chips into the tops before baking them or sprinkle carob shavings or crumbled peanuts on top right after baking, while the biscuits are still a little moist.

Nutritional yeast adds flavor, protein, and important vitamins and minerals. Nutritional yeast is an inactive yeast grown specifically for its great taste and high nutrient content. It can be found in natural food stores or can be ordered from online retailers. (Note: Active dry yeast used for bread baking is not the same as nutritional yeast.)

> 9 cups whole wheat flour
>
> 1 cup nutritional yeast flakes
>
> 1 tablespoon garlic powder *(see note)*
>
> 1 tablespoon salt
>
> 3 cups warm water and/or salt-free vegetable broth

Preheat the oven to 350 degrees F. Combine the flour, nutritional yeast flakes, garlic powder, and salt in a large mixing bowl. Gradually stir in the water, a little at a time. Knead the mixture into a pliable dough; this will take a few minutes. If the dough seems too moist, add a little more flour.

Roll out the dough to a thickness of ¼ to ½ inch. Cut it into the shape of your choice using a cookie cutter or the rim of a drinking glass. Arrange the biscuits on a dry baking sheet and bake for about 15 minutes. Turn the oven off but do not remove the biscuits. Allow the biscuits to cool in the oven for 8 to 12 hours, until they are hard and crunchy.

Stored in sealed containers or zipper-lock bags, Vegan Dog Biscuits will keep for 4 to 5 days at room temperature or 12 months in the freezer.

NOTE: Although raw garlic is toxic to dogs in larger quantities, a small amount used for seasoning is considered safe.

TIPS

- Oil your hands before kneading the dough to keep it from sticking to them.
- Keep a bowl of warm water handy. If the dough becomes too hard to handle, dip your fingers in the warm water and rub them over the dough. This will help to keep the dough pliable.
- Keep extra flour on hand to dust over the rolling surface and the dough if they become sticky.
- If you don't have a rolling pin, use a can of soup or beans.

Bulldog Bulgur Biscuits

YIELD: 50 (3-inch) BISCUITS

These biscuits are high in potassium, iron, and riboflavin. If they were intended for people, they would be considered health food.

3 cups unbleached white flour

3 cups whole wheat flour

2 cups bulgur

1½ cups plain or vanilla soymilk

1 cup cornmeal

3 cups salt-free vegetable broth, as needed

Olive oil or vegetable oil, as needed

Preheat the oven to 300 degrees F. Combine the white flour, whole wheat flour, bulgur, soymilk, and cornmeal in a large mixing bowl. Add 2 cups of the vegetable broth and mix well, using your hands, to make a stiff dough. Add more of the broth as necessary.

On a lightly floured surface, using a floured rolling pin, roll out the dough to a thickness of ¼-inch. Using a 3-inch biscuit cutter or the rim of a drinking glass, cut out the biscuits. Arrange the biscuits on a dry baking sheet. Brush the tops with olive oil and bake for 45 minutes.

Turn the oven off but do not remove the biscuits. Allow the biscuits to cool in the oven for 8 to 12 hours, until they are hard and crunchy.

Stored in sealed containers or zipper-lock bags, Bulldog Bulgur Biscuits will keep for 5 to 7 days at room temperature or 12 months in the freezer.

VARIATION: For extra crunch, sprinkle the tops of the biscuits with bulgur, pressing it in lightly with the palm of your hand, before brushing with olive oil.

Oatmeal and Parmesan Dog Biscuits

YIELD: 20 TO 25 (3-inch) BISCUITS

For a fancier finish, decorate the tops of these treats with additional rolled oats before baking them.

1½ cups very hot water

1 cup rolled oats

¼ cup vegan margarine

½ cup soymilk

½ cup soy parmesan cheese

1 cup cornmeal

1 cup wheat germ

3 cups whole wheat flour plus more as needed

Preheat the oven to 350 degrees F. Combine the water, rolled oats, and margarine in a large mixing bowl. Let stand for 10 minutes to soften the oats.

Stir in the soymilk and soy parmesan cheese. Then add the cornmeal and wheat germ and mix well. Stir in the flour, ⅓ cup at a time, mixing well after each addition. Knead for 3 to 4 minutes, adding additional flour as needed to make a stiff dough. Pat or roll out the dough on a flat surface to a thickness of about ½ inch.

Using a 3-inch biscuit cutter or the rim of a drinking glass, cut out the biscuits. Arrange the biscuits on a dry baking sheet. Bake for about 1 hour.

Turn the oven off but do not remove the biscuits. Allow the biscuits to cool in the oven for 8 to 12 hours, until they are hard and crunchy.

Stored in sealed containers or zipper-lock bags, Oatmeal and Parmesan Dog Biscuits will keep for 5 to 7 days in the refrigerator or 12 months in the freezer.

Main Dishes

You think dogs will not be in heaven? I tell you, they will be there long before any of us.

ROBERT LOUIS STEVENSON

The recipes in this section are ones you can rely on as daily staples for your dog's main meals. Not only are they wholesome and satisfying, they are also easy and fun to prepare. Try making several different kinds and rotating them to give your pooch variety both in taste and nutrition. They can be stored in individual serving sizes in the refrigerator or freezer, so you may want to prepare larger quantities to make mealtime a breeze.

Barking Barley and Wheat Surprise

YIELD: 5 (6-ounce) SERVINGS

For everyday feeding or just a quick meal on a busy day, this is a staple you can always count on. The finished product looks a lot like standard canned dog food. If you like, add any dog-friendly vegetables you have on hand. It's a great way to clear out the fridge!

1 cup cooked barley *(see page 38)*

1 cup whole wheat flour

1 cup firm cooked lentils *(see page 37)*

1 cup salt-free vegetable broth

Preheat the oven to 350 degrees F. Combine the barley, flour, and lentils in a medium casserole dish. Pour the broth over the mixture, cover with a lid, and bake for 45 minutes. Let cool. The surface will look wet, but it will become drier as it stands. Serve warm or at room temperature.

Stored in individual portions in sealed containers or zipper-lock bags, Barking Barley and Wheat Surprise will keep for 5 to 7 days in the refrigerator or 6 months in the freezer.

Snoopy's Great Pumpkin, Rice, and Beans

YIELD: 5 (6-ounce) SERVINGS

This is a nutritious dinner that will have your dogs howling for more. Be sure to buy unsweetened canned pumpkin, not pumpkin pie filling.

1 *(15-ounce)* can pumpkin

1 cup cooked brown rice *(see page 36)*

1 cup cooked or canned red or black beans, rinsed and drained

Combine all of the ingredients in a food processor or blender and process until smooth. Stored in individual portions in sealed containers or zipper-lock bags, Snoopy's Great Pumpkin, Rice, and Beans will keep for 7 days in the refrigerator or 6 months in the freezer.

VARIATIONS

- Sprinkle bulgur over each serving to add some crunch.
- Sprinkle cooled cooked lentils over each serving for added nutrition.

Canine Cashew Casserole

This is a terrific casserole to prepare for visiting dogs or to take to a relative's or friend's home.

1 *(12-ounce)* bag fresh or frozen vegan burger crumbles

1 *(12-ounce)* can vegan mushroom gravy

½ cup grated carrot

½ cup grated potato

½ cup sliced green beans *(fresh, canned, or frozen; if using fresh, remove strings)*

1 stalk celery, diced

¼ cup chopped raw cashews

1 tablespoon garlic powder

4 to 6 strips vegan bacon substitute, chopped

Preheat the oven to 350 degrees F. Place all of the ingredients in a large casserole dish and stir well. Cover and bake for 30 minutes. Remove from the oven, uncover, and let cool.

To cook in the microwave, combine the ingredients in a microwave-safe casserole dish. Microwave on high (100 percent power) for 10 minutes.

Cool completely before serving. Stored in individual portions in sealed containers or zipper-lock bags, Canine Cashew Casserole will keep for 5 days in the refrigerator or 3 months in the freezer.

Oats, Rice, Veggies, and Lentils

This recipe is great for making large amounts ahead of time.

1 bunch broccoli

2 cups rolled oats

1 cup cooked lentils *(see page 37)*

1 cup cooked brown rice *(see page 36)*

1 cup finely grated carrots

1 cup cut green beans, strings removed

1 cup chopped spinach

1 teaspoon garlic powder

Grate the broccoli stems and finely chop the florets. Transfer the broccoli to a large mixing bowl. Add all the remaining ingredients and mix until thoroughly combined.

Stored in individual portions in sealed containers or zipper-lock bags, Oats, Rice, Veggies, and Lentils will keep for 5 to 7 days in the refrigerator or 6 months in the freezer.

Rover's Risotto

This is so delicious, you may want to ask your furry friend if he'll share!

2 cups finely chopped steamed vegetables of your choice

1 *(15-ounce)* can pumpkin

1½ cups cooked brown rice *(see page 36)*

1 cup chopped spinach

Place all of the ingredients in a medium mixing bowl and stir until well combined. Cool before serving.

Stored in individual portions in sealed containers or zipper-lock bags, Rover's Risotto will keep for 5 to 7 days in the refrigerator or 6 months in the freezer.

VARIATIONS

- Sprinkle bulgur over each serving to add some crunch.
- Sprinkle nutritional yeast over each serving for added nutrition.

Fruits, Veggies, and Oats

If your dogs are breakfast eaters like mine, they will love this nourishing treat. If your dog is recovering from surgery or has a wound, substitute kiwifruit for the peaches. Kiwifruit is rich in vitamin C, which is important in wound healing.

    1 banana, mashed

    1 cup unsweetened applesauce

    1 *(15-ounce)* can pumpkin

    1 cup sliced fresh or juice-packed canned peaches

    1 cup mashed cooked or canned sweet potatoes or yams

    2 cups oatmeal *(see page 39)*

Combine the banana and applesauce in a small bowl. Combine the pumpkin, peaches, and sweet potatoes in a large bowl. Add the banana mixture, then stir in the oatmeal and mix well. Cool before serving.

Stored in individual portions in sealed containers or zipper-lock bags, Fruits, Veggies, and Oats will keep for 5 to 7 days in the refrigerator or 6 months in the freezer. Warm the leftovers before serving.

NOTE: To cook sweet potatoes or yams, preheat the oven to 350 degrees F. Scrub them well and pierce them once or twice with the tines of a fork. Place them in a shallow baking pan or directly on the oven rack (with a pan on a lower rack to catch any drippings) and bake for about 1 hour, or until tender. Alternatively, cut the sweet potatoes or yams into chunks and boil them in water until tender.

German Shepherd's Pie

YIELD: 8 (6-ounce) SERVINGS

This is a twist on shepherd's pie, an old Irish standard. Irish Wolfhounds will love it, of course, and so will all other breeds.

1 *(14-ounce)* package firm tofu

1 cup frozen peas and carrots, thawed

1 cup diced potato

1 cup canned vegan brown gravy

2 stalks celery, diced

½ cup sliced fresh or frozen green beans
   (if using fresh, remove strings)

2 cups salt-free vegetable broth

Preheat the oven to 350 degrees F. Combine the tofu, peas and carrots, potato, gravy, celery, and green beans in a large casserole dish. Add the broth and stir until evenly mixed. Cover and bake for 30 minutes. Remove from the oven, uncover, and let cool.

To cook in the microwave, combine all the ingredients in a microwave-safe casserole dish. Microwave on high (100 percent power) for 10 minutes.

Cool completely before serving. Stored in individual portions in sealed containers or zipper-lock bags, German Shepherd's Pie will keep for 3 to 5 days in the refrigerator or 3 months in the freezer.

Chihuahua Chili sans Carne

YIELD: 5 (8-ounce) SERVINGS

This vegan version of Mexican chili is great for your dog. It is high in vitamins B$_6$ and C and riboflavin, potassium, and thiamin.

2 cups diced tofu

1 cup salt-free vegetable broth

1 cup diced zucchini

½ cup cooked brown rice *(see page 36)*

1 flour tortilla, torn into small pieces

½ cup tomato sauce

½ cup shredded carrot

¼ teaspoon chili powder

Place all the ingredients in a large saucepan and stir until well mixed. Cover and simmer on medium heat for about 25 minutes. Strain through a mesh strainer or colander to remove the liquid. (The liquid may be used as vegetable broth in another recipe.) Cool completely before serving.

Stored in individual portions in sealed containers or zipper-lock bags, Chihuahua Chili sans Carne will keep for 5 to 7 days in the refrigerator or 3 months in the freezer.

Special Treats

Outside of a dog, a book is a man's best friend.
Inside of a dog, it is too dark to read.

GROUCHO MARX

Birthdays, holidays, weddings, and funerals that include our canine companions have become big business. People love to celebrate their companion animals and do so by making a big fuss over them on important occasions.

Doggie birthday cakes and gifts are sold at upscale "bowser" boutiques and presented at special pooch parties. Adoption celebrations are held to honor a lucky shelter dog who has finally found a home. The passing of our beloved pets has produced a new wave of "Fido funerals," where other dogs are invited to a repast to pay tribute to their special friend. And at Christmas and Hanukah, dogs are just as likely to be decked out with the colors of the season and receive gifts with their names on them as any other member of the family.

What can you take to these gatherings and what can you feed the canine guests at your own celebrations? This section contains a few ideas for you to try.

Banana-Nut Crunch Bars

YIELD: ABOUT 36 (2-inch) BARS

These bars can be offered as a special treat, or you can arrange them in a lovely gift box for an especially delightful doggy gift.

1½ cups mashed banana

¼ cup peanut butter

¼ cup vegetable oil

2 teaspoons vanilla extract

5 cups oat flour

½ teaspoon baking soda

Water, as needed

Preheat the oven to 325 degrees F. Lightly oil 2 baking sheets.

Place the banana, peanut butter, oil, and vanilla extract in a medium mixing bowl and stir until well blended. Combine the flour and baking soda in a large mixing bowl and make a well in the center. Pour the banana mixture into the well and stir until mixed. Add a little water, 1 tablespoon at a time, to make a kneadable dough. Knead the dough by hand on a flat surface until all the ingredients are well combined.

Form the mixture into 12 strips, each about 6 inches long and 1 inch wide. Cut the strips into 3 equal pieces to make 36 bars. Arrange the bars on the prepared baking sheets and bake for 30 to 40 minutes. Remove from the oven and let cool for at least 20 minutes.

Stored in sealed containers or zipper-lock bags, Banana-Nut Crunch Bars will keep for 7 days in the refrigerator or 12 months in the freezer.

Apple Pupcakes

YIELD: 12 TO 14 CAKES

These can be decorated with carob chips or dusted with a very fine coat of confectioners' sugar for an extra-special treat.

2¾ cups water

1 cup diced apple or chopped dried apples

¼ cup unsweetened applesauce

4 cups whole wheat flour

1 tablespoon cornstarch dissolved in 1 cup warm water

1 tablespoon baking powder

Dash ground cinnamon

Preheat the oven to 350 degrees F. Lightly oil 12 to 14 muffin cups (do not use paper liners).

Combine the water, apple, and applesauce in a large mixing bowl. Add all the remaining ingredients and mix well, scraping the sides of the bowl. Pour evenly into the prepared muffin cups. Bake for 25 minutes, or until a toothpick inserted into center comes out dry. Cool completely before serving or storing.

Stored in sealed containers or zipper-lock bags, Apple Pupcakes will keep for 7 days in the refrigerator or 6 months in the freezer.

Bowser's Birthday Cake

YIELD: 1 (8-inch) LOAF CAKE

Naturally, I had to include a recipe for a tasty vegan birthday cake for your canine companion.

  1½ cups unbleached white flour
  1½ teaspoons baking powder
  1 cup puréed cooked lentils
  1 cup unsweetened applesauce
  ½ cup vegetable oil
  Unsweetened apple butter or confectioners' sugar *(optional)*

Preheat the oven to 325 degrees F. Oil and flour an 8 x 5 x 3-inch loaf pan.

Sift together the flour and baking powder and set aside. Place the lentils, applesauce, and oil in a large bowl. Stir until smooth and well combined. Gradually add the flour mixture and stir to make a smooth batter. Pour into the prepared loaf pan. Bake for 1 hour.

Cool for 10 minutes before removing the cake from the pan. If desired, frost the cake with apple butter or dust it lightly with confectioners' sugar just before serving.

Stored in a sealed container, Bowser's Birthday Cake will keep for 5 to 7 days in the refrigerator or 3 months in the freezer.

Pekingese Pumpkin Pops

YIELD: 18 CUPCAKE-SIZE POPS

Dogs love to chew on frozen items. Even something as effortless as ice cubes can be a refreshing, calorie-free, summer treat for dogs. To make plain ice cubes more exciting, just add bulgur, wheat germ, ripe bananas, puréed pumpkin, cooked lentils, grated carrots, carob chips, apple juice, apple sauce, boxed cereal, or vegan burger crumbles or other faux meat to the water before freezing it into cubes. But for something really special, try this simple recipe. I use standard-size muffin cups for my big dogs, but you may want to use mini-muffin cups or even ice-cube trays for smaller dogs.

> 2 *(15-ounce)* cans pumpkin
> 2 cups plain soy yogurt

Place the pumpkin and yogurt in a large mixing bowl. Stir until well combined. Pour into 18 standard muffin cups and freeze.

Transfer the frozen pops to sealed containers or zipper-lock bags. Pekingese Pumpkin Pops will keep for 12 months in the freezer.

Snickerpoodles

This pooch-popular treat is a twist on the all-time favorite cookie called snickerdoodles.

- 1 cup vegetable oil
- 1 cup molasses
- 1 overripe banana, mashed
- 3½ cups unbleached white flour
- 2 teaspoons cream of tartar
- 1 teaspoon baking soda
- ½ cup cornmeal
- 2 teaspoons ground cinnamon

Preheat the oven to 400 degrees F. Lightly oil 2 baking sheets.

Place the oil, molasses, and banana in a large mixing bowl. Mix until well combined. Add the flour, cream of tartar, and baking soda and knead into a well-blended dough.

Combine the cornmeal and cinnamon in a small bowl. Scoop the dough by rounded teaspoonfuls and shape into balls. Roll the balls in the cornmeal mixture, coating them well all over. Place the balls 2 inches apart on the prepared baking sheets and press them down with a fork. Bake for 8 to 10 minutes. Cool completely before serving.

Stored in sealed containers or zipper-lock bags, Snickerpoodles will keep for 7 days in the refrigerator or 12 months in the freezer.

Cheese Dog Delights

YIELD: MAKES 30 SERVINGS

These cheesy biscuits are sure to be a crowd pleaser and are a fun project for a rainy day. Sprinkle them with soy parmesan cheese or soy cheddar for an extra-cheesy snack.

1 cup whole wheat flour

½ cup cornmeal

8 ounces soy cream cheese

2 tablespoon vegetable oil

1 tablespoon nutritional yeast flakes

1 teaspoon vegetable bouillon powder

Soy parmesan cheese or soy cheddar *(optional)*

Preheat the oven to 350 degrees F. Combine the flour, cornmeal, soy cream cheese, oil, nutritional yeast flakes, and vegetable bouillon powder in a food processor and process until well combined. Press the mixture onto a large baking sheet to about 1 inch thick. Sprinkle with soy parmesan cheese, if desired.

Bake for 45 minutes. Remove from the oven and cut into bite-size squares. Lower the oven temperature to 200 degrees F. Continue baking for 1 hour. Cool completely before serving.

Stored in sealed containers or zipper-lock bags, Cheese Dog Delights will keep for 5 to 7 days in the refrigerator or 6 months in the freezer.

Hound Dog Delights

YIELD: 40 (2- to 3-inch) BISCUITS

These rich, flavorful cookies make a lovely gift arranged in a pretty basket with a chew toy or two. Use your imagination and try a variety of cookie-cutter shapes.

6 cups all-purpose flour

1 cup water

½ cup vanilla soy coffee creamer

¼ cup carob chips, melted

¼ cup molasses

2 tablespoons olive oil

2 tablespoons vegan margarine

1 tablespoon brown sugar

1 tablespoon peanut butter

Preheat the oven to 350 degrees F. Lightly oil 2 baking sheets.

Place all the ingredients in a large mixing bowl. Stir until well combined to make a dough. Cover and chill the dough in the refrigerator for 1 hour.

Roll half the dough on 1 of the baking sheets. Cut it into the shapes of your choice, and then remove the surrounding dough. Roll and cut the remaining dough on the other baking sheet. Bake for 1 hour. Turn the oven off but do not remove the biscuits. Allow the biscuits to cool in the oven for 8 to 12 hours, until they are hard and crunchy.

Stored in sealed containers or zipper-lock bags, Hound Dog Delights will keep for 5 to 7 days in the refrigerator or 6 months in the freezer.

Puppy Party Hors D'oeuvres

YIELD: 12 TO 25 COOKIES

These are great little snacks for a puppy party or for everyday treats for your special dog. They make great training treats as well; just make them very small.

1 *(12-ounce)* bag vegan burgers crumbles

1 cup finely grated carrot

½ cup bread crumbs

¼ cup unsweetened applesauce

1 tablespoon shredded soy cheese

2 teaspoons garlic powder

1 teaspoon salt-free tomato paste

Preheat the oven to 350 degrees F. Lightly oil a baking sheet.

Place all the ingredients in a medium mixing bowl. Mix until thoroughly combined. Roll into balls (larger balls for larger dogs, smaller ones for smaller dogs).

Arrange on the prepared baking sheet and bake for 15 minutes, or until firm and golden brown. Cool completely before serving.

Stored in sealed containers or zipper-lock bags, Puppy Party Hors D'oeuvres will keep for 7 to 10 days in the refrigerator or 12 months in the freezer.

Peanut Butter Banana Treats

YIELD: 18 TO 24 (2-inch) COOKIES

Dogs love peanut butter. You can't go wrong with these cookies.

1 cup unbleached white flour

1/2 cup soymilk

1/4 cup soy parmesan cheese

1/4 cup mashed banana

2 tablespoons peanut butter

1 teaspoon baking powder

1 tablespoon water

Preheat the oven to 400 degrees F. Lightly oil a baking sheet.

Combine the flour and soymilk in a large bowl and stir until lumpy. Mix in the soy parmesan cheese. Add the banana, peanut butter, and baking powder. Then stir in water and mix well. Add more water as necessary until the mixture is the consistency of cake batter.

Spoon the batter onto the prepared baking sheet to form cookies; each cookie should be about 2 inches in diameter. Bake for 20 minutes, or until brown. Turn the oven off but do not remove the cookies. Allow the cookies to cool in the oven for 8 to 12 hours, until they are hard and crunchy.

Stored in sealed containers or zipper-lock bags, Peanut Butter Banana Treats will keep for 5 to 7 days in the refrigerator or 6 months in the freezer.

Resources

Nutritional Information

Vegan Action
www.vegan.org

Vegan Dog Nutrition Association
www.vegandognutritionassociation.com

Vegetarian Dogs
www.vegetariandogs.com

Vegan Dog Food, Biscuits, and Kibble

The Celestial Shop
www.thecelestialshop.com
415-588-1733

Natural Life Pet Products
www.nlpp.com
800-367-2391

Evolution Diet
www.petfoodshop.com
800-659-0104

V-dog
www.v-dogfood.com
888-280-8364

Harbingers of a New Age
www.vegepet.com
406-295-4944

Vegan Essentials
www.veganessentials.com
800-88-VEGAN

Mail Order Catalog
www.healthy-eating.com
800-695-2241

West Coast Pet Supply
www.westcoastpetsupply.com
800-604-2263

Index

Recipe Notes

Recipe Notes

Recipe Notes

Recipe Notes

BOOK PUBLISHING COMPANY

since 1974—books that educate, inspire, and empower

To find your favorite vegetarian and alternative health books online, visit:
www.healthy-eating.com

Also by Michelle Rivera

Living in Harmony with Animals
Carla Bennett
978-1-57067-084-8 $9.95

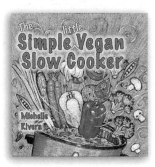

The Simple Little Vegan Slow Cooker
978-1-57067-071-5 $9.95

Cooking with PETA
People for the Ethical Treatment of Animals
978-1-57067-044-2 $14.95

Local Bounty
Devra Gartenstein
978-1-57067-084-8 $17.95

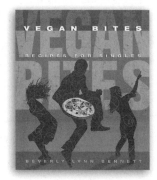

Vegan Bites
Beverly Lynn Bennett
978-1-57067-221-7 $15.95

Purchase these health titles and cookbooks from your local bookstore or natural food store, or buy them directly from:

Book Publishing Company • P.O. Box 99 • Summertown, TN 38483 • 1-800-695-2241

Please include $3.95 per book for shipping and handling.